The Lost Destiny

Tamara Vella

BookLeaf
Publishing

India | USA | UK

Presentation by *BookLeaf Publishing*

Web: www.bookleafpub.com

E-mail: info@bookleafpub.com

ISBN:9789358314489

First edition 2023

The Dragon

In the realm where legend stirs,
Amongst the shroud of mystery,
There exists a beast, gloriously mighty,
Born of fire from a distant land.

Scales glinting with forgotten hues,
Eyes bearing ancient secrets, deeply spoken,
Roars that ricochet from mountain to mountain,
Striking a deep fear into all creatures' hearts.

Wings unfurled, it dances with the wind,
A silhouette against the twilight's canvas,
Navigating the boundless expanse,
A dance between earth and sky,
In the symphony of existence, it thrives.

In each scale, a story etched deep,
Histories of empires, dreams and sleep,
An emblem of untamed strength and mythical
might,
An eternal embodiment of the ages gone by.

The Siren

In the moon's cold, unfeeling embrace, she
emerges,
A siren of the abyss, her beauty but a facade,
Her song, a harrowing dirge of dark allure,
Drowning souls within the icy depths, enslaved.

Amidst the inky blackness, her presence chills,
A spectral figure, draped in tattered shrouds,
Her voice, a malevolent whisper that instills,
Fear and dread in those who hear her haunting
sounds.

Her eyes, like voids where light dare not tread,
Conceal the hunger for lost souls, a hunger never
fed,
In her song, the lament of the forever dead,
She's a temptress of doom, where horror spreads.

A siren, a harbinger of malevolence and pain,
In her wake, life's purity forever wanes,
In the crushing depths, where the lost remain,
She's a creature of darkness, where no light
remains.

The Goblin

Where darkness meets mischief, he comes to
play,
The goblin, a creature from the hollows of a
world unseen with gnarled limbs,
With wrinkled skin like leather, scarred and
grey,
And emerald eyes that glitter, a mischievous
glint in their depths.

The goblin, a creature from the hollows of a
world unseen with gnarled limbs,
Wearing a tattered cloak, threads like spider's
silk,
And emerald eyes that glitter, a mischievous
glint in their depths,
As he dances through the moon's silvery milk.

Wearing a tattered cloak, threads like spider's
silk,
His spindly fingers trace symbols in the air,
As he dances through the moon's silvery milk,
Leaving traces of enchantment in his lair.

His spindly fingers trace symbols in the air,

With wrinkled skin like leather, scarred and grey,
Leaving traces of enchantment in his lair,
Where darkness meets mischief, he comes to play.

The Will-o'-the-Wisps

Will-o'-the-wisps, in the heart of the night's
embrace,
Dance with lanterns of molten gold, a celestial
grace,
They twinkle and beckon with otherworldly
delight,
Guiding souls through a realm of mystical
might.

In marshes and moors, where the darkness is
deep,
They lead with a promise, secrets they keep,
With a luminous glow, like stars on a cosmic
shore,
They tempt and they tease, forevermore.

Oh, will-o'-the-wisps, your mystique astounds,
In your ethereal realm, where wonder knows no
bounds,
You illuminate the path, a celestial display,
Guiding wanderers through twilight's enchanting
array.

Yet, heed the allure of their celestial ballet,
For in their radiant dance, reality may sway,

In the heart of the night, where dreams weave and swell,
The will-o'-the-wisps conjure a magical spell.

The Baku

In the realm where night and dreams entwine,
A mystical Baku, guardian of twilight's sigh,
Emerges as moonlight's secret confidante,
Unseen by mortal eyes in the shrouded night,
In whispers, it lends its ethereal aid,
Guiding dreamers through the realms where
secrets play.

The Baku's presence, where the mystical secrets
play,
In a dreamscape where moonbeams intertwine,
A spectral guide with ancient, silent aid,
Serving the seekers of the midnight sky,
In the tapestry of dreams, under night's veil so
tight,
With every breath, it is the moon's confidante.

As starlight weaves its tales, a celestial
confidante,
The Baku stirs the realm where fantasies play,
With a touch of magic, their visions take flight,
And woven threads of destiny they entwine,
A nocturnal ballet in the velvet night,
Under its watchful gaze, the dreams receive aid.

In the hush of night, when mysteries require aid,
The Baku becomes the dreamer's confidante,
Whispering secrets, where moonbeams ignite,
In the theater of slumber, where reveries play,
Boundless as the constellations that entwine,
Within the ethereal tapestry of the mystical
night.

A guardian of enigma, in the embrace of night,
The Baku serves as the dreamer's silent aid,
Guiding through the realms where visions
entwine,
Unveiling the esoteric, it is the dreams'
confidante,
Dancing amidst the stars where fantasies play,
In the moon's tender luminescence, their secrets
ignite.

In this mystical realm, where dreamers seek aid,
The Baku emerges, a celestial confidante,
In the nocturnal symphony, where destinies
entwine,
In the sanctuary of dreams, under night's
embrace,
As the stars, like enchanted whispers, gently
play,
Beneath the moon's soft glow, their secrets
ignite.

The Kitsune

Amidst a sea of cherry blossoms' grace,
A kitsune roams with an alluring face,
Her fur, a flame of crimson and pure white,
Eyes like emeralds in the soft spring light.

Nine tails of silver, like ribbons that sway,
Her figure elegant in Sakura's array,
In the season of blooms, she is the queen,
A kitsune's presence, a sight to be seen.

She moves with grace, her spirit gleaming
bright,
A guardian of blossoms, in the hush of the night,
In the heart of Sakura, a vision of charm,
The kitsune's beauty, beneath the blossoms' arm.

The Kraken

In the depths where no light reaches,
A behemoth stirs, an ocean's leviathan,
A kraken, a titan of the boundless abyss,
Emerging from the watery shadows.

Its colossal form, an undulating mass,
Scales like midnight, a monstrous embrace,
Unfurls, as it reaches for a hapless ship,
Engulfed by its serpentine, writhing arms.

The ship, once a vessel of human endeavor,
Now becomes a toy in the kraken's grasp,
Wood creaks and groans as the behemoth rises,
Carrying its stolen prize into the depths.

The crew's cries are silenced in the inky void,
Their ship's destiny bound to the kraken's whim,
In the heart of the ocean, where secrets reside,
The kraken reigns, a force both dark and grim.

The Basilisk

In the heart of a cavern, beneath earth's cascade,
A basilisk dwells, in the shadows' serenade,
With scales like shadows, a glint of emerald
green,
In the cave's depths, its venom's unseen.

A basilisk dwells in the heart of the cave,
Its hiss a whisper, in the echoes it'll engrave,
In the cavern's depths, its venom's unseen,
A creature of wonder, in the moon's soft sheen.

Its hiss, a whisper, in the echoes it'll engrave,
Its eyes like jewels, in the darkness they guide,
A creature of wonder, a serpent, serene,
In the moon's soft glow, it remains a mystery
unseen.

Its eyes like jewels, in the darkness they guide,
With scales like shadows, a glint of emerald
green,
In the moon's soft glow, it remains a mystery
unseen,
In the heart of the cavern, where secrets and
danger coincide.

For if one's gaze should meet this basilisk's dread,
Its venomous death would surely be spread,
To look upon its form, a fatal embrace,
In the heart of the cavern, where death takes its place.

The Chimera

A creature of ancient myths, born of chaos,
Chimera's form, a tapestry of discordant parts,
Lion's body, serpent's tail, a goat's defiance,
A fusion of nature's whims and mystic arts.

In her eyes, the stories of countless eras,
A guardian of secrets, both dark and divine,
Each breath she takes stirs a tempest of terror,
Yet within her, a labyrinth of enigma lies.

A chimera's being, a paradox of nature's strife,
In the realm of dreams, she leads a curious life,
Her existence, a riddle, a marvel of creation's
dance,
In the tapestry of legends, she's given her
chance.

The Sphinx

A Sphinx with eyes like blazing suns,
In desert's embrace, he waits and runs,
Half lion's grace, half human's gaze,
To travellers, his riddle he conveys.

With a body of sandstone, ancient and grand,
In his stoic posture, he guards the land,
With wings that cast a shadow vast,
His enigmatic riddle is the traveller's task.

In the shimmering heat of the desert's haze,
He asks his question, his voice ablaze,
A puzzle to solve, a challenge to embrace,
To pass the Sphinx's test and continue the race.

His face, a visage of regal pride,
With strength and wisdom, side by side,
In the land of sands, where time has its say,
The Sphinx stands guard, by night and by day.

To the traveller who dares the desert's domain,
He presents a conundrum, a mental terrain,
His riddle, a test of wit and resolve,
For those who seek the secrets his words
involve.

The Gorgon

In solitude, the gorgon seeks her fate,
A creature born with snakes for flowing hair,
With eyes that turn all they gaze upon to stone,
Her beauty's curse, a sorrowful lament.

With each encounter, fear and evil loom,
Her heart aches for a love that's kind and true.

Her visage marred by the curse that's all too true,
In seeking love, she battles against fate,
But often, those she meets bring only gloom,
For no one can look past her snaky hair,
To see the tenderness her eyes lament,
Her quest for love amid a world so stone.

Her tears fall hot as molten lava stone,
An agony that speaks of her deepest truth,
A soul in need of love, in endless lament,
She longs to rewrite her forsaken fate,
To be seen beyond her writhing hair,
And find a heart untouched by dark and gloom.

But in her world, where darkness reigns with
gloom,

She finds few willing to embrace a heart of
stone,
To hold her close and touch her snaky hair,
To love the gorgon, see the hidden truth,
And together, they'd defy the cruel hand of fate,
But in despair, her heart remains lament.

In shadows cast by the moon's lament,
She wanders through a world veiled in gloom,
A lonely gorgon, battling the hand of fate,
Her touch turns all to unforgiving stone,
Yet yearning for a love that's pure and true,
To caress her cheek and twine her snaky hair.

In dreams, a love who'll see beyond her hair,
To soothe her with a love devoid of lament,
To prove that in her, goodness can be true,
To pierce the darkness, dispel the heavy gloom,
To face her gaze and not turn into stone,
To rewrite the script of her ill-fated fate.

The gorgon seeks a love that defies her fate,
Hoping to find someone who'll comb her hair,
With tender touch, dispelling the curse of stone,
To heal her heart, ending her endless lament,
Together they'd conquer the deepest gloom,
A love that's pure, bound by a bond that's true.

The Vampire

In the still of the night, deep where moonlight's
fingers creep,
A vampire stalks its prey with eyes aglow,
Its form, a creature from the realms below,
Invisible whispers through the darkness seep.

With skin like alabaster, kissed by the moon,
Eyes fiery orbs that pierce the darkest sleep,
It moves with grace, in silence, slinking low,
Seeking the warmth of life, its secrets keep.

Sharp fangs concealed, behind lips stained
blood-red,
A predator, with grace and deadly charm,
From the shadows, its prey it soon will claim.

The Cerberus

Cerberus, three-headed hound of blackest night,
With eyes like burning coals, a fearsome blight,
Guardian of the gates to realms of dread,
Infernal warden, where lost souls are spread.

Each head with jaws agape, a savage snarl,
No hope or light in their unceasing snarl,
A sentinel of Hades, fierce and cruel,
To cross its path means entering the tomb's rule.

Infernal realms' tormentor, dark and vile,
Cerberus stands with eyes like death's own guile,
No mortal dare defy its wicked reign,
For in its presence, all know endless pain.

A creature born of malevolence and despair,
Cerberus guards the underworld's grim lair.

The Griffin

Amidst Himalayan peaks, the yeti stands,
Its massive form, a creature of the snow,
With fur as white as the untouched ice,
In these remote heights, where mysteries grow.

In solitude, it roams with shaggy coat,
A silent guardian, in the bitter cold,
Its eyes like ancient glaciers, deep and remote,
A creature of myth, a legend's stronghold.

With every echoing howl, the mountains sing,
A haunting song in these frigid heights,
In this barren realm, where legends cling,
The yeti's presence, a living enigma's rights.

In caverns dark, it finds its sheltered berth,
The yeti's den, in the frozen earth's embrace,
A world untamed, where curiosity's worth,
In the Himalayan depths, a timeless place.

Through frosty gusts, the Himalayas sing,
Their echoes holding stories intertwined,
In the heart of these heights, the yeti's king,
A legend's form, where myths are enshrined.

Amidst the peaks, where legends meet the snow,
A yeti's spirit, in every story's flow.

The Unicorn

A unicorn's grace,
Pearlescent coat and eyes bright,
In moonlight's embrace,
A creature of pure delight,
Innocence in every stride.

The Thunderbird

The Thunderbird, its feathers fierce and bold,
With eyes that spark, like lightning's vibrant
thread,
In skies of power, its presence takes its hold,
A creature of the tempest, where legends are
spread.

With eyes that spark, like lightning's vibrant
thread,
Each wingbeat shakes the heavens, fierce and
grand,
A creature of the tempest, where legends are
spread,
In its mighty grasp, it wields the storms'
command.

Each wingbeat shakes the heavens, fierce and
grand,
The Thunderbird, with powers vast and
untamed,
In its mighty grasp, it wields the storms'
command,
A guardian of the skies, in myth, it's named.

The Thunderbird, its feathers fierce and bold,

In skies of power, its presence takes its hold,
A guardian of the skies, in myth, it's named,
With powers vast and untamed, forever
acclaimed.

The Banshee

In the veil of night, a banshee's eerie cry,
A mournful sound, with secrets long concealed,
Her form, a phantom in the pale moon's light,
She wanders through the realm of dreams and
dread.

With long, flowing hair, like shadows in the
night,
She weaves her tale, where mortal fears reside.

Her presence veiled in darkness, where fears
reside,
A wailing banshee with her mournful cry,
She roams the hours of the moonlit night,
In the ancient lore, her essence is concealed.

Her eyes, like emerald orbs, in the night,
Gleam with a spectral and ghostly light.

A figure of the dark, with ethereal light,
She whispers secrets where the shadows reside,
Her cry, a dirge that pierces through the night,
A mournful banshee's call, a ghostly cry.

In the depth of legends, her truth is still
concealed,
A phantom's presence in the haunting night.

She lingers in the depths of the eerie night,
A banshee's grace, a spectral, ghostly light,
In tales of old, where mysteries are concealed,
Among the spirits and the phantoms that reside,
A mournful cry, a banshee's fateful cry,
In the echoes of time, where legends take flight.

Her song reverberates through the endless night,
A banshee's haunting cry, a siren's light,
In the hearts of those who in the legends reside,
A creature veiled in secrets, hidden from sight.

In the weave of stories, where her secrets are
concealed,
A banshee's lament in the midst of the night.

A banshee's cry, a mournful sound in the night,
In the tapestry of myths, where legends reside,
Her form concealed, her presence veiled in light,
She remains a mystery, in the deep of the night.

The Phoenix

In the ashes of time, the phoenix does rest,
A symphony of flames, a fiery test,
From embers, it rises, a creature reborn,
In each dawn's first light, its spirit adorned.

With feathers aglow in hues of vivid flame,
Each plume an artwork, a radiant frame,
Its wings stretch wide, a tapestry reborn,
In each dawn's first light, its spirit adorned.

Its beak of ebony, its eyes ablaze with light,
A regal creature in the midst of night,
In the dance of the flames, its soul takes flight,
A phoenix reborn, in the eternal light.

From ashen slumber, it emerges with grace,
Resurrected beauty in this sacred space,
From the depths of despair, it finds its morn,
In each dawn's first light, its spirit reborn.

The Fenrir

In the shadowed realms of myth, Fenrir waits,
A wolf of darkest night, with eyes ablaze,
His ebony fur, a shroud of moonless skies,
A creature born of fear, of age-old cries.

In monstrous form, his fangs like jagged spears,
A terror in the hearts of those who hear,
His eyes, like burning coals, searing and fierce,
In the depths of dread, his presence will pierce.

Fenrir, a nightmare in the realm of old,
A creature fierce and wild, a story told,
In tales of darkness, where legends are spun,
The wolf of doom, in shadows, he's become.

The Manticore

A manticore with wings, a vile design,
Eyes of malevolence in a body malign,
A creature of darkness, ruthless in its quest,
In the shadows it prowls, a relentless, wicked
jest.

Eyes of malevolence in a body malign,
Claws sharp as daggers, in the darkest design,
In the shadows it prowls, a relentless, wicked
jest,
Its venomous tail poised, to pierce and infest.

Claws sharp as daggers, in the darkest design,
No mercy it offers, in its cruel incline,
Its venomous tail poised, to pierce and infest,
A creature of evil, in the night it invests.

No mercy it offers, in its cruel incline,
A manticore with wings, a creature malign,
A creature of evil, in the night it invests,
In the heart of darkness, where terror rests.

The Cyclops

In mythic tales of old, a Cyclops fierce and
grand,
With one eye wide and raging, a solitary sentinel
stands,
His towering form a titan, his skin like
weathered sand.

In its single eye, a tempest brews, fury like fire's
demand,
The depths of its anger, a force hard to
understand,
In the epic sagas, it's known as the guardian of
the land.

A single eye, fierce and unyielding, in a world
so unmanned,
Through legends and stories, its wrath, an
enduring brand,
In the heart of the myth, a Cyclops, mighty and
unplanned.

As ancient tales unfurl, his image across the ages
spanned,
With a single eye aflame, in myth, he's a figure
so in command,

In its furious gaze, the essence of a world
forever damned.